BABY GROUND SQUIRREL

Published in Canada by Fitzhenry & Whiteside, 195 Allstate Parkway, Markham, Ontario L3R 4T8
Published in the United States by Fitzhenry & Whiteside, 121 Harvard Avenue, Suite 2, Allston, Massachusetts 02134

10 9 8 7 6 5 4 3 2 1

National Library of Canada Cataloguing in Publication Data
Lang, Aubrey
Baby ground squirrel / text by Aubrey Lang ; photography by Wayne Lynch
(Nature babies)
ISBN 1-55041-797-5 (bound).—ISBN 1-55041-799-1 (pbk.)
1. Ground squirrels—Infancy—Juvenile literature. I. Lynch, Wayne
II.Title.   III. Series: Lang, Aubrey. Nature babies.
QL737.R68L36 2003   j599.36'5   C2002-905292-0

U.S. Cataloging-in-Publication Data
(Library of Congress Standards)
Lang, Aubrey.
Baby ground squirrel / text by Aubrey Lang ; photography by Wayne Lynch. — 1st ed.
[32] p. : col. photos. ; cm.   (Nature babies)
Includes bibliographical references and index.
Summary: Winter is barely over when the baby ground squirrels (also known as the prairie gopher) are born. At first completely dependent on their mother, the little ones will grow up quickly. By midsummer their parents will disappear underground again to snooze the rest of the season away. And now the young ones face the world alone, as they fatten themselves up for the long winter ahead.
ISBN 1-55041-797-5
ISBN 1-55041-799-1 (pbk.)
1. Squirrels — Juvenile literature. [1. Squirrels.] I. Lynch, Wayne, 1948- . II. Title. III. Series.
599.36 [E] 21   2003 CIP

Fitzhenry & Whiteside acknowledges with thanks the Canada Council for the Arts, the Government of Canada through the Book Publishing Industry Development Program (BPIDP), and the Ontario Arts Council for their support for our publishing program.

Design by Wycliffe Smith Design Inc.
Printed in Hong Kong

Baby Ground Squirrel

Text by Aubrey Lang

Photography by Wayne Lynch

Fitzhenry & Whiteside

BEFORE YOU BEGIN

Hello Young Reader,

We love to watch and photograph baby animals. We wrote this book to share with you some of the secrets in the life of a family of ground squirrels.

To photograph the ground squirrels in this book, we spent three years watching them in a colony very close to our home on the edge of Calgary, a large city in Western Canada. We always hid inside a small tent, called a blind. The ground squirrels never knew we were there.

We dedicate this book to biologist and ground squirrel researcher Dr. Gail Michener, and to landowner Sam Mahood.

— Aubrey Lang and Wayne Lynch

TABLE OF CONTENTS

For many years the ground squirrels have lived in the farmer's field behind the big red barn. Every winter the field is quiet and empty. The squirrels hibernate deep below the frozen ground where they spend the winter months alone, buried inside a bundle of dry grasses. Soon it will be spring in Western Canada, and the squirrels will be active again.

A hibernating male squirrel is curled up with his nose tucked between his legs. His body feels almost frozen and he hardly breathes. If you poked him with your finger, nothing would happen. You could even roll him on the ground like a furry bowling ball.

One day the squirrel shivers and twitches. He slowly uncurls. He warms up, checks the weather, and decides it is time to come outside. The squirrel's hibernation is over for another year.

Even though there is still snow on the ground, it's a warm day in early spring. Male squirrels, like this one, are the first to dig out of their burrows. The females are still hibernating. The male is nervous, and he peeks above the snow, searching for hungry predators. When it is safe, he sneaks outside into the sunshine and nibbles on dry grasses.

He uses his long front claws to scratch through the crusty snow.

Hundreds of ground squirrels live together in the farmer's field, so there are usually many eyes to watch for danger. When a squirrel spots an owl or a flying hawk, it gives a special chirp and they all escape underground. If they see a badger, a coyote, or even the friendly farmer, the danger signal is different—a loud whistle.

Sniff, sniff. Sniff, sniff. There's a new lady ground squirrel in the field, and the male has found her. At first she runs away, but the excited male follows her. They spend the afternoon together, and later they go down into her burrow. He will be the father of her new babies, but she will raise them by herself.

In three weeks, the mother ground squirrel has five new babies. Also known as a "pinkie", each baby is the size of your thumb. The tiny squirrels have big heads and mouths so they can suckle and drink lots of milk. They use their strong front legs and tiny claws to crawl through the grassy nest. When they find their brothers and sisters, the little ones snuggle together to stay warm.

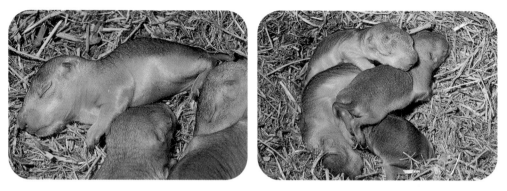

The babies are now ten days old. Their ears have grown and they are starting to look more like little squirrels. But they still cannot see.

During the day, the mother leaves the babies alone so she can search for food. With so many pups to feed, the mother is always hungry. She munches on juicy grasses and flowers to satisfy her appetite.

The babies are always hungry. They chirp and chirp and chirp, like noisy little birds. The mother comes back to the family burrow many times during the day to nurse her growing pups. When mother comes home, the babies push and shove and climb over each other to reach her milk. Now that the pups are bigger, the nursery gets crowded at mealtime.

Although the pups are now eighteen days old, they have never left the small underground nursery where they were born. The nursery is part of the family burrow, which has several other rooms, including a special toilet room. Underground tunnels connect the rooms. Inside the nursery it is dark all the time. The pups don't know when it is day or night.

For several days the baby squirrels have been exploring the tunnels inside their burrow. This morning they crawl all the way to the surface. Three pups squeeze out of one hole; two squeeze out of another.

The month-old pups are easily frightened. When a large black-and-white bird lands nearby, they dive underground. A daring young female peeks outside to see where the scary bird has gone, but the harmless magpie has flown away.

Now that her babies no longer need to nurse, the mother gets a welcome rest. The young squirrels eat lots of grass. Crunchy grasshoppers are also a favorite meal.

The youngsters love to play. They follow colorful lady-bugs and bumblebees. They chew on feathers and sticks. They tumble and wrestle, and play endless games of tag.

The little female, like her brothers and sisters, is always itchy. Her fur is full of biting fleas. She nibbles and scratches, but she can't get rid of the itch.

Suddenly the sharp-eyed female sees an animal moving through the grass. She stands as tall as she can to see it better. Then she runs to a hole and whistles an alarm. The colony is in great danger.

A badger is the ground squirrel's worst enemy. It's a dangerous digging machine with powerful claws and razor-sharp teeth. It digs faster and deeper than any ground squirrel can.

The badger runs to the burrow where the squirrel family lives. It digs furiously. The terrified ground squirrels run through their tunnels in all directions. When the badger isn't looking, the sneaky squirrels get away through secret holes. This time the badger loses.

It's the end of summer. The young female is very fat, and almost as big as her mother, who is now hibernating. Although she will stay in the colony, the female will take over some of the burrow for herself. She gathers mouthfuls of grass to build a warm, dry nest underground. Soon she will hibernate for the winter, alone in her burrow.

Next spring she will raise a family of her own.

DID YOU KNOW?

- The squirrels in this book are Richardson's ground squirrels of the northern prairies. Many people call them gophers. They are also called "picketpins" and "flickertails".

- A ground squirrel is different from a tree squirrel. The eyes of a ground squirrel are high on its head to help detect flying predators. It has small ears, which trap less dirt when the animal tunnels. Its claws are long and adapted for digging. A tree squirrel, on the other hand, has eyes on the sides of its head, large ears, and sharp claws designed for climbing.

- In a ground squirrel colony, each adult female has her own burrow. But she is not alone. She lives surrounded by close female relatives, such as her mother, daughters, sisters, and aunts.

- A typical ground squirrel burrow has 5 to 7 surface entrances and as many as 5 sleeping chambers that can be up to 39 inches (1 meter) deep. The network of tunnels may be 33 feet (10 meters) long.

- Adult males live only one or two years, while adult females live three or four. Males die sooner because they fight each other fiercely during the spring mating season. Many juvenile males also die when they leave the colony in mid to late summer, and move away to distant colonies.

- Adult ground squirrels are active above ground for as short a time as possible to lessen the risk from predators. So once the breeding season is over, they hibernate as soon as they fatten up. On average, adult males enter hibernation in early June while adult females wait until early July. The juveniles, who must finish growing, enter hibernation later; juvenile females enter in the middle of August, and juvenile males wait until the end of September.

- During the many months of hibernation, a squirrel does not eat or drink but lives on its fat reserves. It arouses and rewarms its body for a few days every three to four weeks, but the squirrel remains underground.

INDEX

BIOGRAPHIES

When Dr. Wayne Lynch met Aubrey Lang, he was an emergency doctor and she was a pediatric nurse. Five years after they were married, they left their jobs in medicine to work together as writers and wildlife photographers. For almost twenty-five years they have explored the great wilderness areas of the world — tropical rainforests, remote islands in the Arctic and Antarctic, deserts, mountains, and African grasslands.

Dr. Lynch is a popular guest lecturer and an award-winning science writer.

He is the author of almost twenty titles for adults and children. He is also a Fellow of the internationally recognized Explorers Club, and an elected Fellow of the prestigious Arctic Institute of North America.

Ms. Lang is the author of eleven nature books for children. She loves to share her wildlife experiences with young readers, and has more stories to tell in the Nature Baby Series.

The couple's impressive photo credits include thousands of images published in over two dozen countries.